EASY PIANO

Disney Songs FOR KIDS

ISBN 978-1-5400-9740-8

Visit Hal Leonard Online at
www.halleonard.com

Contact us:
Hal Leonard
7777 West Bluemound Road
Milwaukee, WI 53213
Email: info@halleonard.com

In Europe, contact:
Hal Leonard Europe Limited
42 Wigmore Street
Marylebone, London, W1U 2RN
Email: info@halleonardeurope.com

In Australia, contact:
Hal Leonard Australia Pty. Ltd.
4 Lentara Court
Cheltenham, Victoria, 3192 Australia
Email: info@halleonard.com.au

CONTENTS

8 The Bare Necessities
THE JUNGLE BOOK

15 Candle on the Water
PETE'S DRAGON

12 Circle of Life
THE LION KING

18 Cruella de Vil
ONE HUNDRED AND ONE DALMATIANS

24 Evermore
BEAUTY AND THE BEAST (2017)

30 Ev'rybody Wants to Be a Cat
THE ARISTOCATS

21 If I Didn't Have You
MONSTERS, INC.

32 Let It Go
FROZEN

35 Never Smile at a Crocodile
PETER PAN

38 Remember Me
(Lullaby)
COCO

40 Show Yourself
FROZEN 2

49 A Spoonful of Sugar
MARY POPPINS

54 Strong
CINDERELLA (2015)

60 That's How You Know
ENCHANTED

66 Touch the Sky
BRAVE

73 When Will My Life Begin?
TANGLED

78 A Whole New World
ALADDIN

86 You'll Be in My Heart*
(Pop Version)
TARZAN®

81 You're Welcome
MOANA

92 You've Got a Friend in Me
TOY STORY

SONG NOTES

The Bare Necessities

This upbeat tune is sung by Baloo and Mowgli in the 1967 film *The Jungle Book*. The passing notes in the left-hand part give this song its energetic feel. Notice measures 8, 16, 20, and similar, and highlight the left-hand part while sustaining the longer notes in the melody. Lean into the syncopation; the half note often falls on beat two for a slightly accented feel.

Candle on the Water

From the 1977 hybrid live-action and animated film *Pete's Dragon*, this Academy Award-nominated song is sung by the character Nora. Play in a legato style, connecting one note to the next. This is a moderately slow ballad; don't be afraid to take some time to shape the phrases, building in intensity through to the last line, where the direction *rit. e dim* means to play slower and softer until the end.

Circle of Life

Written by Elton John with lyrics by Tim Rice, this dramatic song famously opens both the 1994 film version *The Lion King* and the subsequent Broadway production that debuted in 1997. The left-hand rhythm gently propels the melody forward, so find that groove right from the beginning. Note the repeat signs. The 1st ending is played the first and third times, while the 2nd ending is played the second and fourth times, with instrumental measures on the last repeat.

Cruella de Vil

Sung by the character Roger Radcliff in the 1961 animated film *One Hundred and One Dalmatians*, this jazzy tune is lots of fun to play. "Swing" the eighth notes as designated by this symbol ♪♪ = ♩♪ at the beginning of the song, giving them a bouncy "long-short" feel. Look out for accidentals (sharps and flats not in the key signature) throughout. They give a bit of color and dash to this song.

Evermore

This dramatic ballad is sung by the Beast in the 2017 live-action remake of the animated film *Beauty and the Beast*. Set the stage with a legato introduction and allow for some freedom when phrasing the vocal line. Sing along as you consider where you would like the melody to push and pull, listening for tension and release in the harmony, as in measures 24–26, and similar places. Let the story of love and longing unfold and build in intensity before the final four measures bring you to a quiet end.

Ev'rybody Wants to Be a Cat

This fun group number, sung by Scat Cat, Thomas O'Malley, Russian Cat, Duchess, and Marie is featured in the 1970 animated film *The Aristocats*. Keep things lively with the jazzy harmony and a swinging melody. Keep the tempo moderate and the beat steady. With all that syncopation, "everybody" wants to be a cat!

If I Didn't Have You

Sung as a duet by characters Sulley and Mike, this sweet and funny tune is featured in the 2001 Disney • Pixar animated film *Monsters, Inc.* Look out for accidentals in both right and left-hand parts. Accidentals appear in the music as sharps and flats that are not part of the key signature and add interest and color to the harmony. The melody is syncopated, so keep a steady beat and write in any tricky rhythms you find as you play through the song the first few times.

Let It Go

This dramatic anthem is sung by the character Elsa (voiced by Idina Menzel) in the 2013 mega-hit animated film *Frozen*. For this abridged arrangement, choose a tempo that moves steadily, but not too slow. The slanted lines you see between treble and bass clef show the melody moving from right hand to left hand. Play with a full, confident tone, building to the dramatic chorus.

Never Smile at a Crocodile

Written for the 1953 animated film *Peter Pan*, this song was heard without lyrics whenever the Crocodile appeared. After the film was released this sung version became a Disney classic. The left-hand part imitates a "tick-tock" of the clock, so keep it steady. You might try testing yourself by playing with the metronome. The small dots over and under the notes designate *staccato*, which means to play with a lightly detached sound.

Remember Me
(Lullaby)

Sung in various styles, "Remember Me" is the featured song in the 2017 Disney•Pixar animated film *Coco*. This arrangement is sung as a lullaby by the character Hector, to his daughter Coco when he travels far away. It also appears in the film in a mariachi style, and in a pop version over the end credits. "Gently" is a helpful word when deciding on the tempo of this song. Play the right-hand part with a singing, *legato* tone, and let the left-hand notes gently rock back and forth as a simple accompaniment.

Show Yourself

The character Elsa sings this powerful ballad of discovery in the 2019 film *Frozen 2*. Learn this arrangement in sections, careful to note the key changes and accidentals throughout. The melody includes a quarter-note triplet rhythm. Here, the quarter-note triplet takes the time of a half note. Though the time signature is $\frac{4}{4}$, play with a feeling of two pulses per measure, allowing the triplet to fill one of those pulses.

A Spoonful of Sugar

Included in one of the most classic film scores ever, "A Spoonful of Sugar" was written for the 1964 film *Mary Poppins*. Don't rush the opening, marked "Freely." Take your time before you settle into a bright and upbeat tempo by measure 8. From measure 17, the left hand helps keep things steady and moving along in a half-note rhythm. The harmony changes, but the anchor note D stays the same from measure to measure throughout the song.

Strong

Sung over the end credits in the 2015 live-action adaptation of the animated film *Cinderella*, "Strong" is a gentle but powerful ballad. The ₵ time signature signifies a feeling of 2, so lean into the syncopation created by the tied notes in the right-hand melody to keep things moving forward. Listen for all the notes to sound exactly together beginning in measure 15, and emphasize the moving eighth notes in right hand, echoed by left hand in measures 17–18. Keep building through the coda, right through to the dramatic ending.

That's How You Know

Hailed by critics as the best song in the movie, "That's How You Know" was sung by Amy Adams in the 2007 Disney film *Enchanted*. Have fun with the calypso beat beginning in measure 8. Both hands play the same notes just two octaves apart. Knowing this gives you a chance to concentrate on the rhythm. Count and play at a slow tempo first, then relax and enjoy the groove.

Touch the Sky

This stirring ballad appears in the 2012 Disney•Pixar computer-animated fantasy film *Brave*. The story is set in the Scottish Highlands, and you can hear that sense of place expressed right away in the $\frac{6}{8}$ opening section. The time signature changes to $\frac{3}{4}$ in measure 9, where the lyrics begin. The left-hand 5ths support the melody. Play those strongly, but don't overpower the melody. The tempo is indicated as "Quickly" so play this arrangement with plenty of energy and movement.

When Will My Life Begin?

Sung by the character Rapunzel in Disney's 2010 animated feature film *Tangled*, this Broadway-style song leads you through a dizzying description of how the princess spends her days. Play the running 16th notes slightly detached, almost as if you were speaking them, and don't be afraid to accent the syncopation in both hands beginning in measure 16. From measure 34 to the end, take your time, letting the lyrics be your guide.

A Whole New World

Sung as a duet between Aladdin and Jasmine, this romantic ballad is heard in the 1992 animated film *Aladdin*. The melody is syncopated but play gently, listening for a legato sound. Notice the movement from G♯ to G-natural in places like measures 7–8. Lean on the G♯ for a bit of harmonic color, then relax as you play the G-natural. The slanted lines between the staff show that the melody moves to the bass clef for the lower G in the melody.

You'll Be in My Heart*
(Pop Version)

Written and sung by pop artist Phil Collins, "You'll Be in My Heart" is from the 1999 Disney animated feature *Tarzan*. As you begin to learn this song, take note of the interesting rhythms in left hand. Look ahead for several key changes. The song begins in F, with B-flat in the key signature. In measure 21 you move to D major, with F♯ and C♯. Notice the B♭ in parentheses at the end of measure 37. That's a reminder that when you return to the sign, 𝄋, you're back in the original key. In the coda the key changes again, and you play in G major until the end of the song.

You're Welcome

The mighty demigod Maui sings this song in the 2016 feature film *Moana*. You'll need some energy to keep the almost rap-like lyrics moving along. Two things can be helpful here. First, try singing along as you play, looking for repeated notes, and noticing when the melody moves up and down the scale by step. Second, determine the interval distance when the melody leaps higher and lower. For example, find all the places the melody leaps an octave, and notice that the interval is almost always a 6th when Maui sings the lyrics, "You're welcome."

You've Got a Friend in Me

This friendly tune is the theme song in the 1995 Disney•Pixar animated film *Toy Story*. It's also heard in all the *Toy Story* sequels. Syncopation in the melody and chromatic notes in the harmony give this song its unique sound. Keep a steady beat throughout, but let the right hand swing a little, leaning into the ties and dotted notes.

The Bare Necessities

from THE JUNGLE BOOK

Words and Music by
TERRY GILKYSON

Brightly

Look for the bare ne - ces - si - ties, the

sim - ple bare ne - ces - si - ties; ___ for - get a - bout your

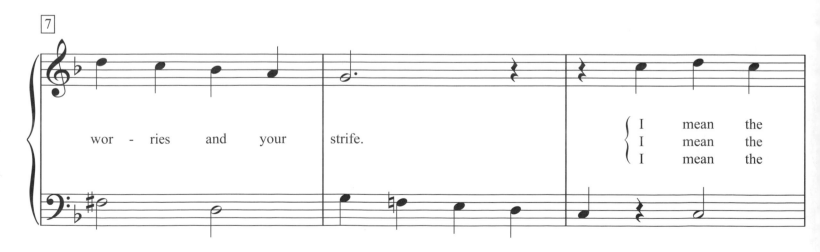

wor - ries and your strife.

I mean the
I mean the
I mean the

fond - er ____ of my big home.
raw paw, ____ next time be - ware.
bee acts ____ you're work - in' too hard.

The bees are buzz - in' in the tree to make some
Don't pick the prick - ly pear by paw, when you pick a
Don't spend your time just look - in' a - round for some-thing you

hon - ey just for me. You look un - der the
pear, try to use the claw. But you don't need ___ to
want that can't be found. When you find out you can

rocks and plants and take a glance at the fan - cy ants, ___ then
use the claw when you pick a pear of the big paw - paw. ___ Have I
live with - out it and go a - long not think - in' a - bout ___ it. I'll

Circle of Life
from THE LION KING

Music by ELTON JOHN
Lyrics by TIM RICE

From the day we ar - rive ___ on the plan - et ___ and
There's far too much ___ to take in here, ___ more to

Instrumental

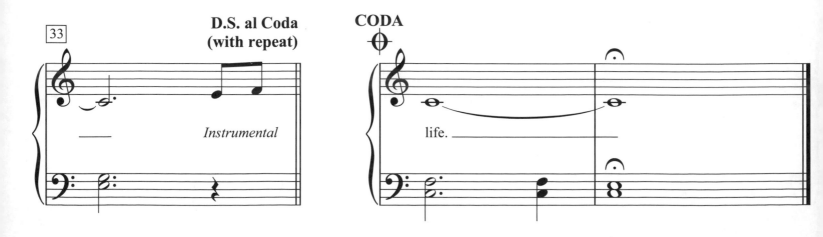

Candle on the Water

from PETE'S DRAGON

Words and Music by AL KASHA
and JOEL HIRSCHHORN

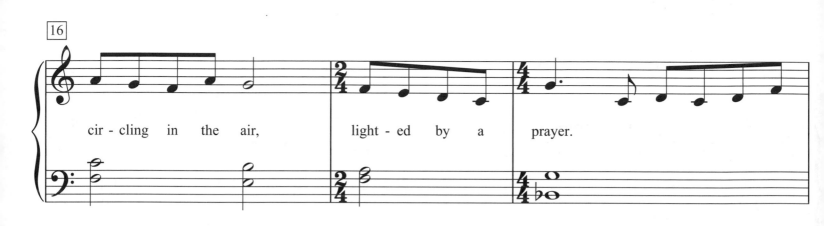

here's my hand so take it. Look for me reach-ing out to show, as sure as riv - ers

flow, I'll nev - er let you go.

I'll nev - er let you go, I'll nev - er let you

go. *rit. e dim.*

Cruella de Vil

from ONE HUNDRED AND ONE DALMATIANS

Words and Music by
MEL LEVEN

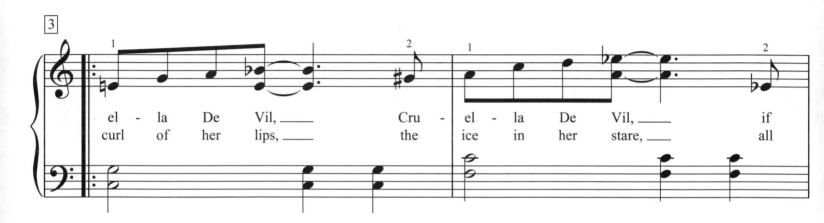

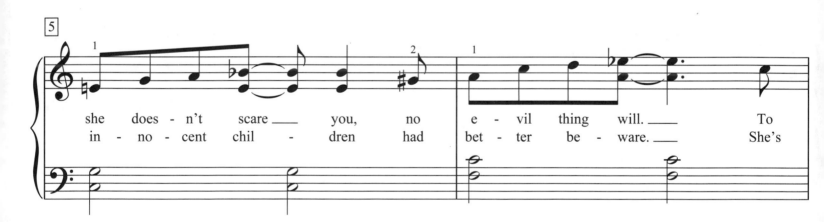

19

rock.   This   vam - pi - re   bat, ____   this

21

in - hu - man   beast, ___   she   ought   to   be   locked ___ up   and

23

nev - er   re - leased. ___   The   world   was   such   a   whole - some   place   un -

25

til   Cru - el - la,   Cru - el - la   De   Vil.

If I Didn't Have You

from MONSTERS, INC.

Music and Lyrics by
RANDY NEWMAN

Ev - 'ry - one loves ___ you, you know. ___ *Sulley:* Yes, I

know, I know, I know. *Mike:* But I must ad - mit it,

big guy, you al - ways come through. I would-n't have

noth - ing if I did - n't have you. ___

Evermore

from BEAUTY AND THE BEAST (2017)

Music by ALAN MENKEN
Lyrics by TIM RICE

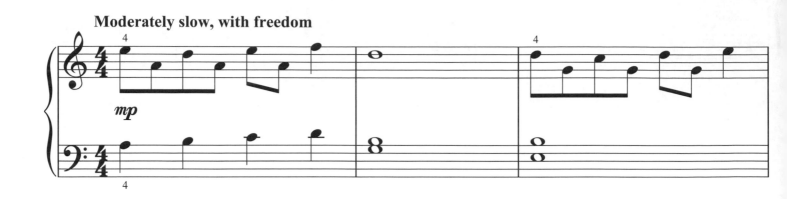

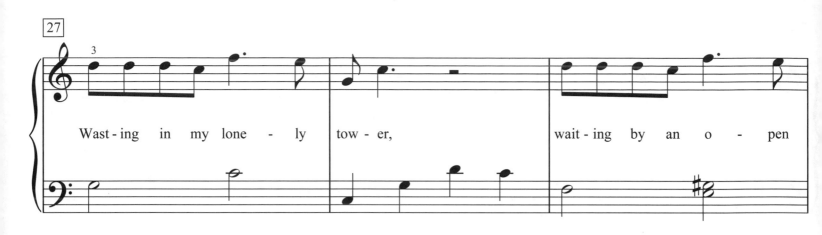

I rage a-gainst the trials of love. I curse the fad-ing of the

light. Though she's al-read-y flown so far be-yond my reach,

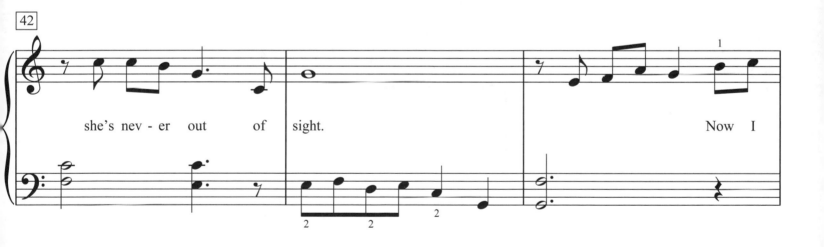

she's nev-er out of sight. Now I

know she'll nev-er leave me, e-ven as she fades from

view. She will still in - spire me, be a part ___ of

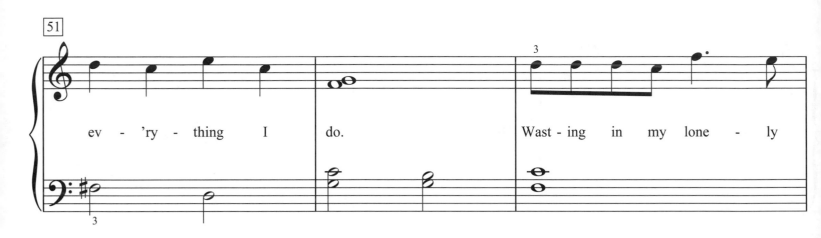

ev - 'ry - thing I do. Wast - ing in my lone - ly

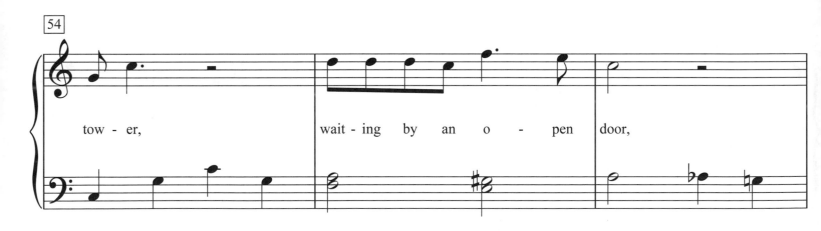

tow - er, wait - ing by an o - pen door,

I'll fool my - self she'll walk right in,

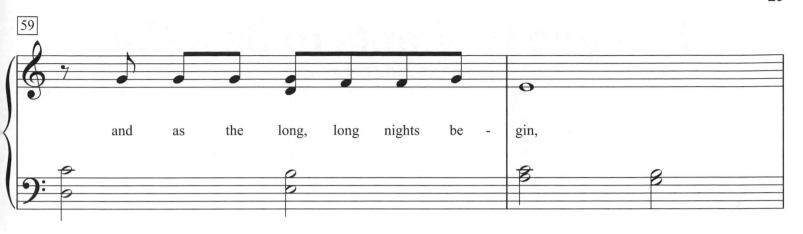

and as the long, long nights be - gin,

I'll think of all that might have been, wait - ing

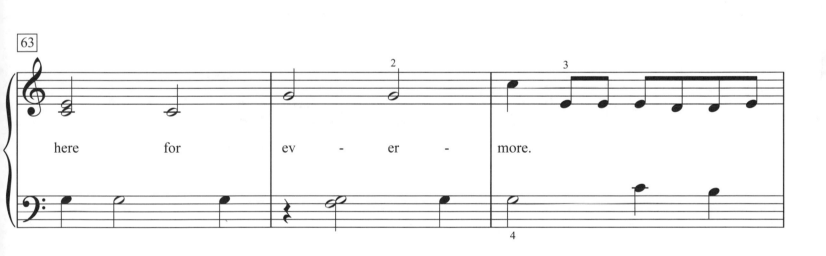

here for ev - er - more.

Ev'rybody Wants to Be a Cat

from THE ARISTOCATS

Words by FLOYD HUDDLESTON
Music by AL RINKER

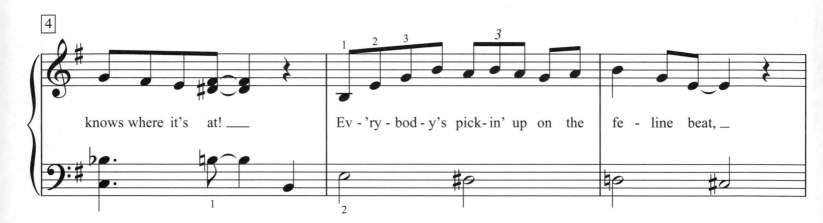

has-n't been tried, ___ I sug - gest you pro - vide ___ your own cat - nip. ___

I've heard some corn - y birds who tried to sing, but still a

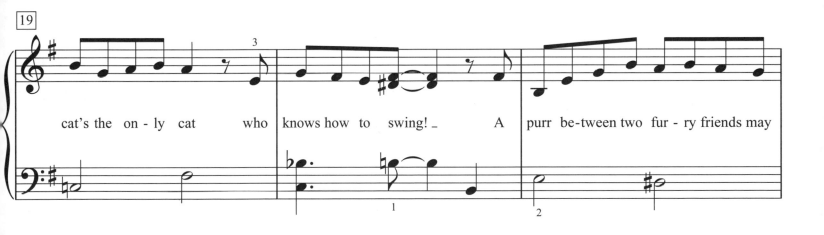

cat's the on - ly cat who knows how to swing! ___ A purr be-tween two fur - ry friends may

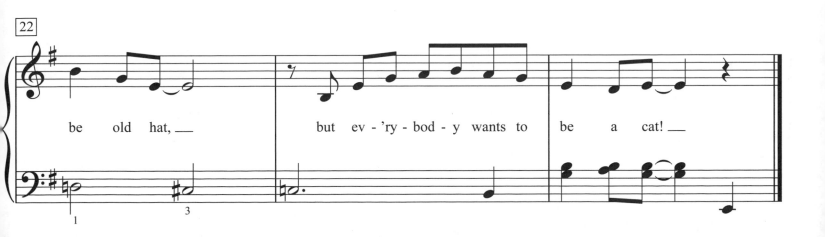

be old hat, ___ but ev - 'ry - bod - y wants to be a cat! ___

Let It Go

from FROZEN

Music and Lyrics by KRISTEN ANDERSON-LOPEZ
and ROBERT LOPEZ

Half-time feel

The snow glows white on the moun-tain to-night, _ not a foot-print _ to be seen. _

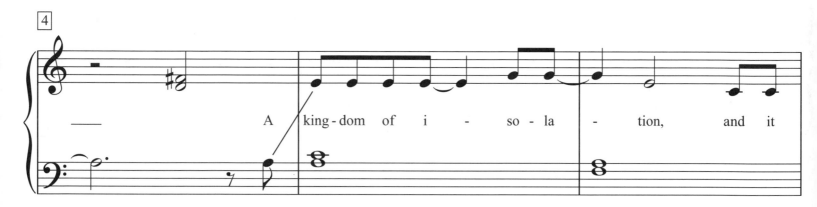

_ A king-dom of i - so - la - tion, and it

looks like I'm the queen. _ The wind _ is howl-ing like this

swirl-ing storm in - side. _ Could-n't keep it in, _

_____ heav-en knows I _____ tried. Don't let _____ them

in, don't let them see, be the good girl you al - ways have to

be. Con - ceal, don't feel, don't let them know... Well, now _

_____ they know. _____ Let it go, _____ let it go, _____ can't _

hold it back an-y-more. ____ Let it go, ____ let it go, ____

____ turn a-way ____ and slam ___ the ___ door. ___ I don't ___ care ___

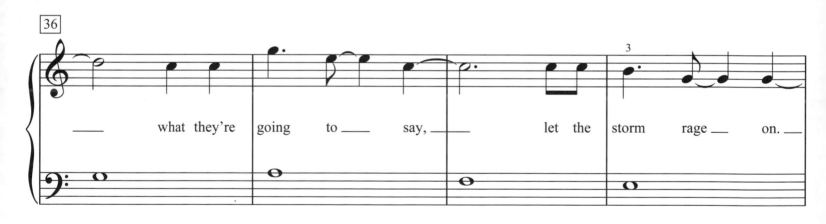

___ what they're going to ____ say, ___ let the storm rage ___ on. ___

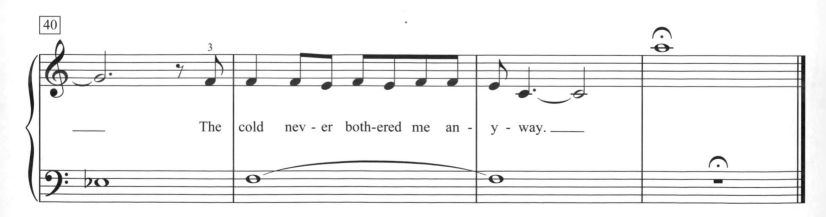

___ The cold nev-er both-ered me an-y-way. ____

Never Smile at a Grocodile

from PETER PAN

Words by JACK LAWRENCE
Music by FRANK CHURCHILL

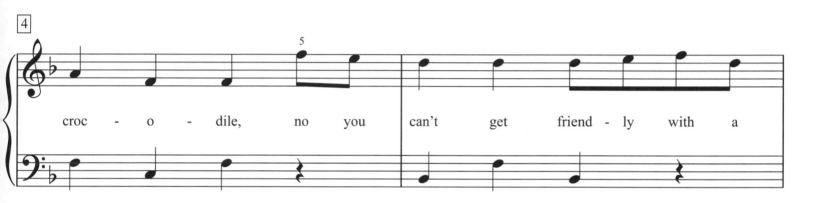

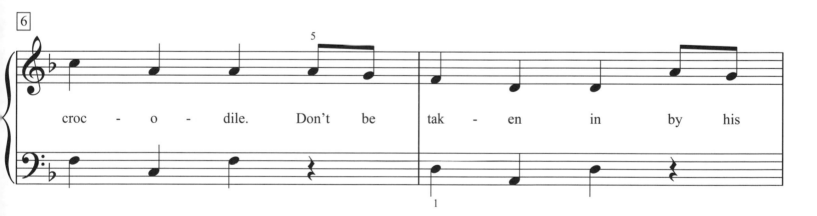

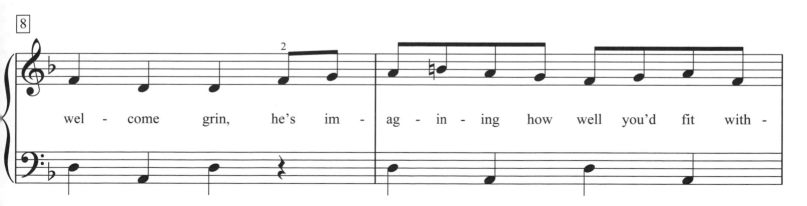

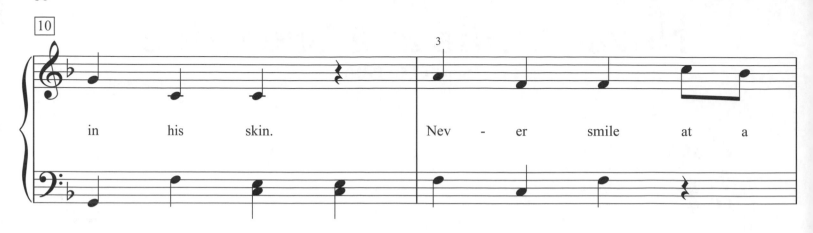

in his skin. Nev - er smile at a

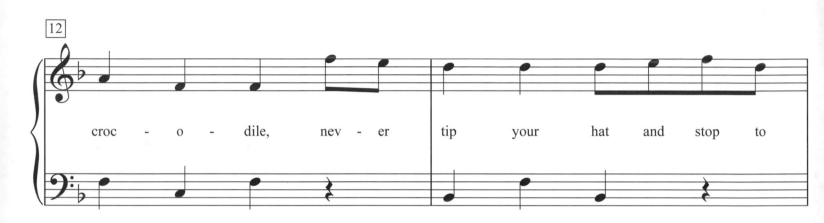

croc - o - dile, nev - er tip your hat and stop to

talk a while. { Nev - er run, walk a - way. Say, "Good -
Don't be rude, nev - er mock, throw a

To Coda ⊕

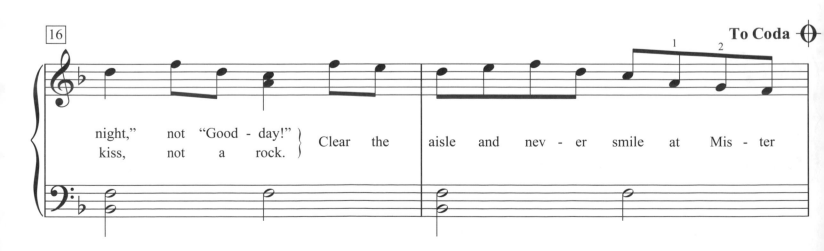

night," not "Good - day!" } Clear the aisle and nev - er smile at Mis - ter
kiss, not a rock.

Remember Me
(Lullaby)
from COCO

Music and Lyrics by KRISTEN ANDERSON-LOPEZ
and ROBERT LOPEZ

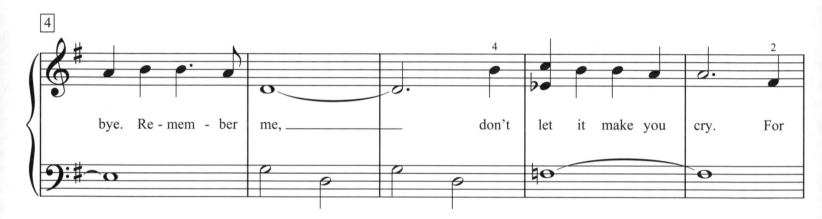

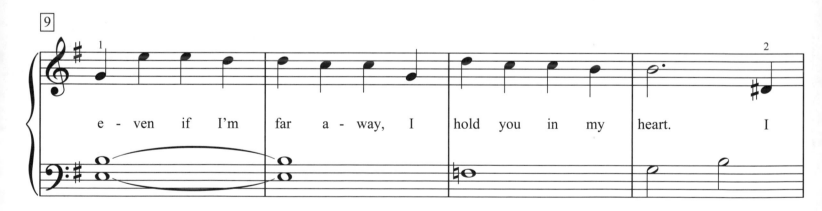

me, _____ though I have to trav - el far. Re - mem - ber

me _____ each time you hear a sad gui - tar.

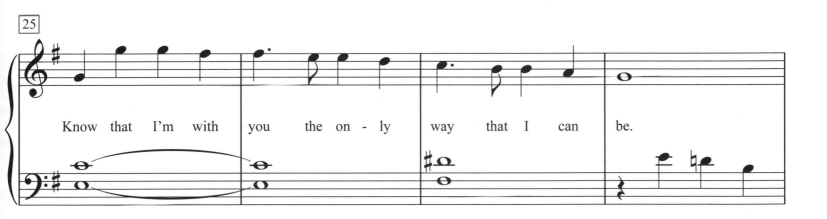

Know that I'm with you the on - ly way that I can be.

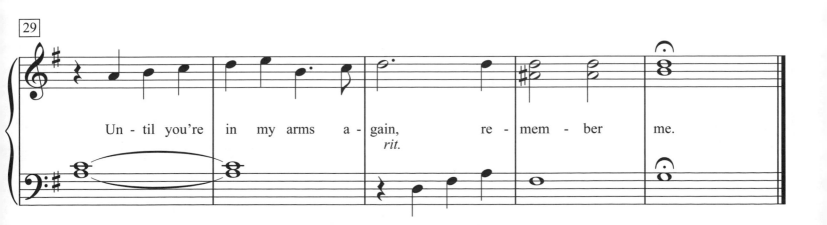

Un - til you're in my arms a - gain, re - mem - ber me.

rit.

Show Yourself

from FROZEN 2

Music and Lyrics by KRISTEN ANDERSON-LOPEZ
and ROBERT LOPEZ

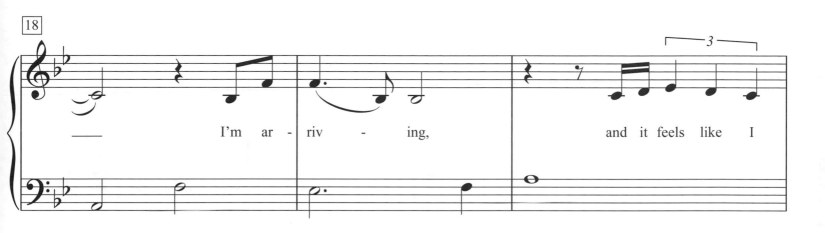

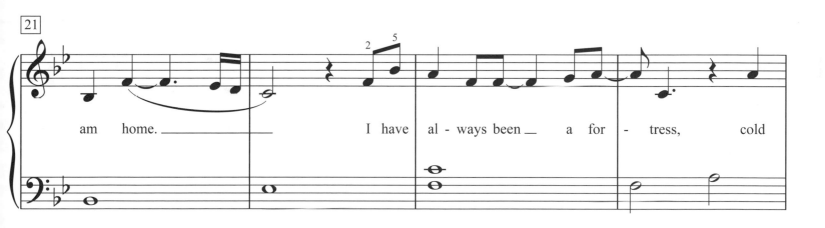

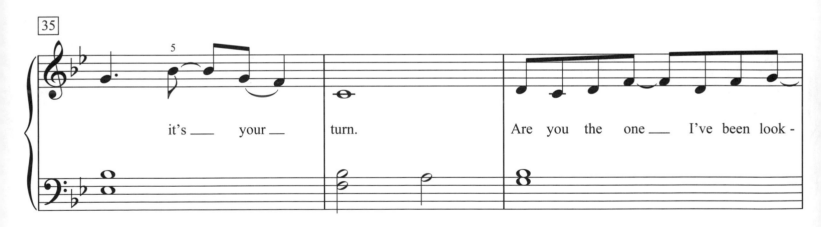

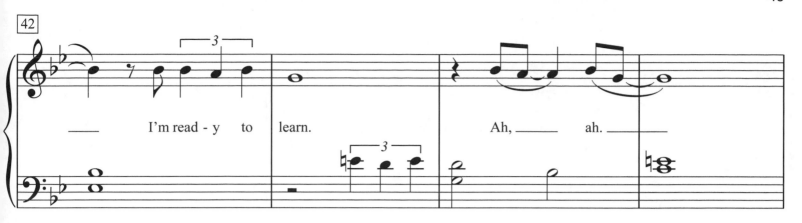

I'm read - y to learn. Ah, _____ ah. _____

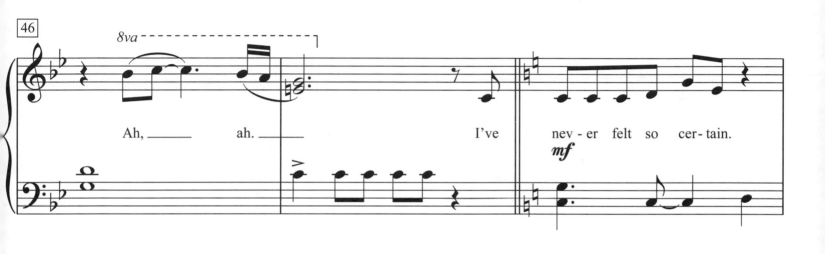

Ah, _____ ah. _____ I've nev - er felt so cer - tain.

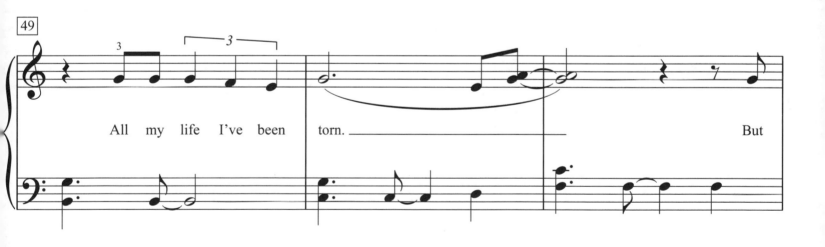

All my life I've been torn. _____ But

I'm here for a rea - son: could it be the rea - son I _____ was born? _

I have al - ways been __ so dif - f'rent. Nor - mal

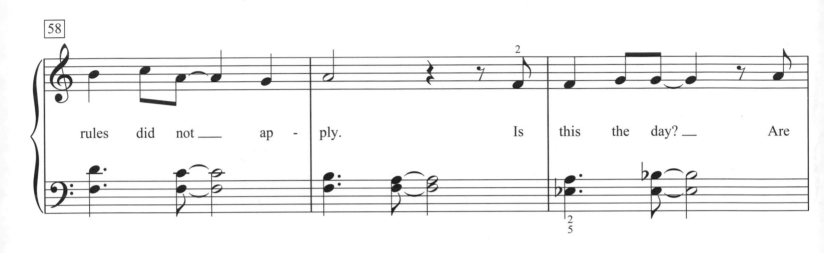

rules did not __ ap - ply. Is this the day? __ Are

you the way __ I fi - n'lly find __ out why? __

Show your - self! I'm no __ long - er trem - bling! Here I __ am: __

Don't make _ me _ wait one mo - ment more! Oh, _

cresc. poco a poco

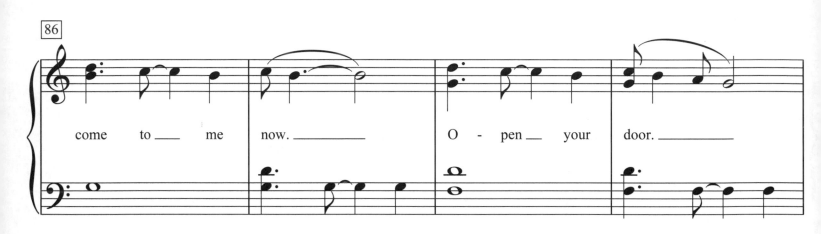

come to _ me now. _____ O - pen _ your door. _____

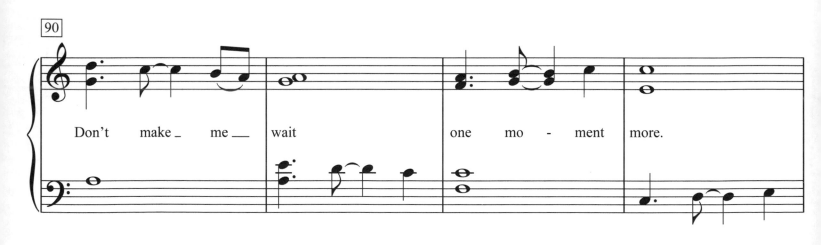

Don't make _ me _ wait one mo - ment more.

rit. (Where the

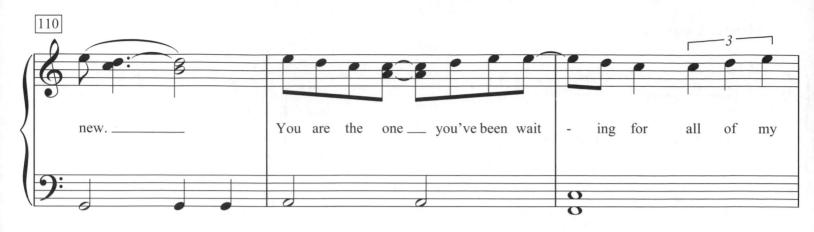

new.＿＿＿ You are the one＿ you've been wait - ing for all of my

life.＿＿＿＿＿ Oh, show your - self!＿＿＿

Ah,＿＿＿ ah.＿＿ Ah,＿＿＿ ah.＿＿

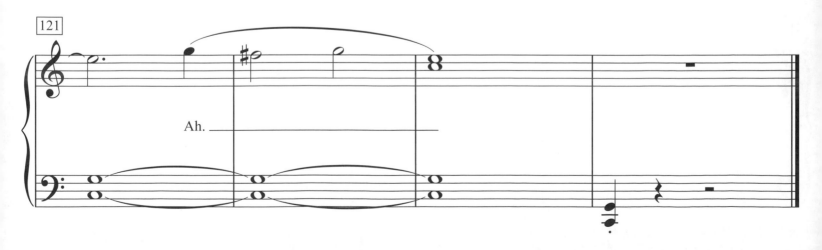

Ah.＿＿＿＿＿

A Spoonful of Sugar

from MARY POPPINS

Words and Music by RICHARD M. SHERMAN
and ROBERT B. SHERMAN

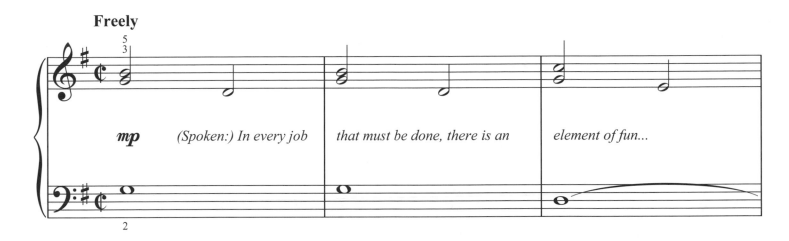

take be - comes a piece of cake, a

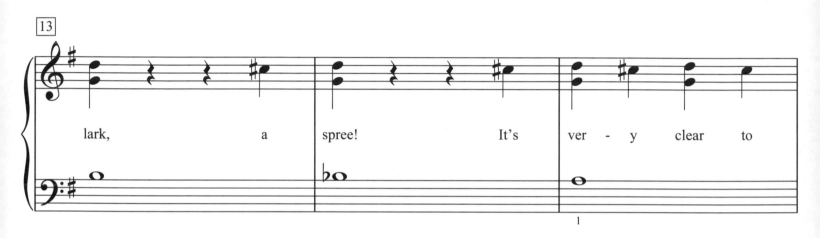

lark, a spree! It's ver - y clear to

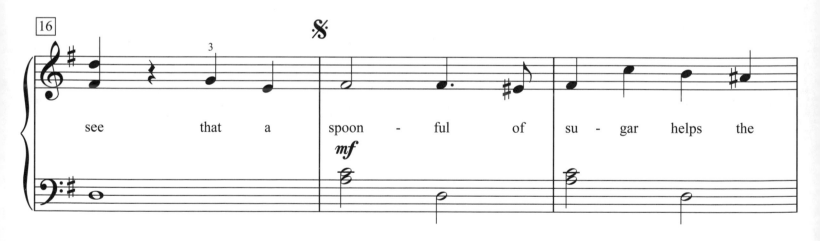

see that a spoon - ful of su - gar helps the

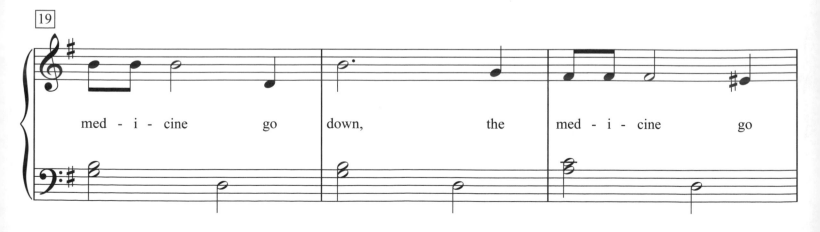

med - i - cine go down, the med - i - cine go

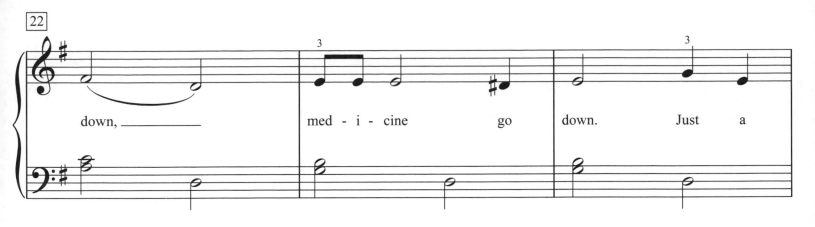

down, _____ med - i - cine go down. Just a

spoon - ful of su - gar helps the med - i - cine go

To Coda ⊕

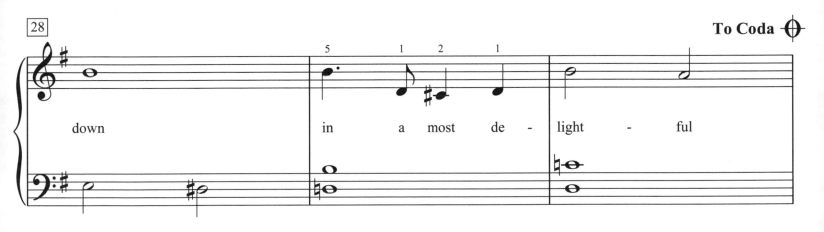

down in a most de - light - ful

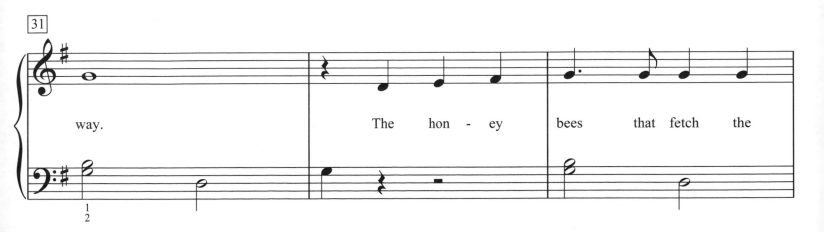

way. The hon - ey bees that fetch the

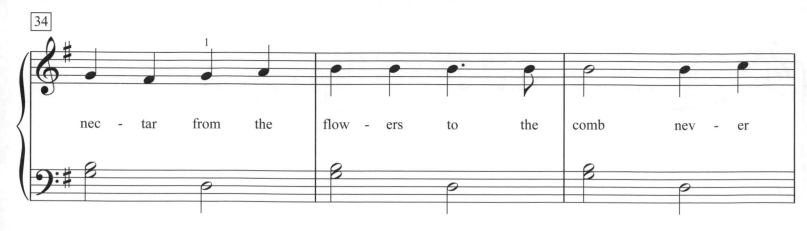

34

nec - tar from the flow - ers to the comb nev - er

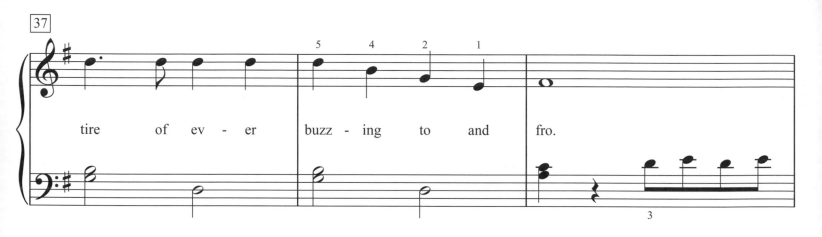

37

tire of ev – er buzz – ing to and fro.

40

Be - cause they take a lit – tle nip from ev - 'ry

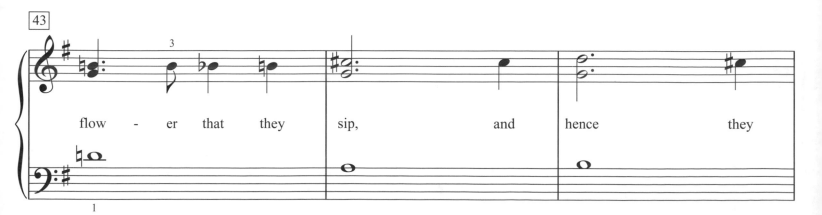

43

flow – er that they sip, and hence they

find their task is not a grind. For a

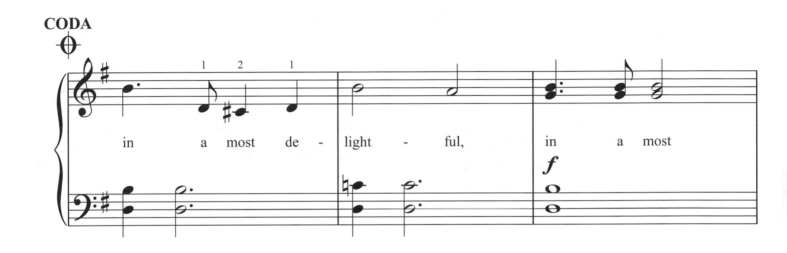

in a most de- light- ful, in a most

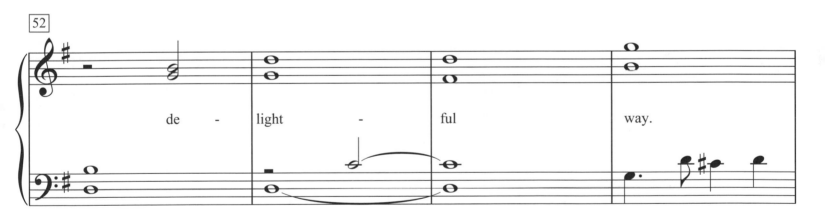

de- light- ful way.

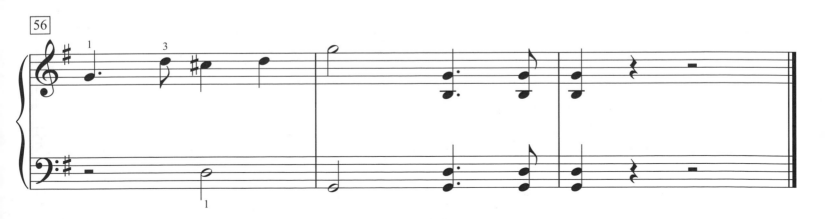

Strong

from CINDERELLA (2015)

Words and Music by PATRICK DOYLE,
KENNETH BRANAGH and TOMMY DANVERS

soul shines _ for - ev - er and ev - er. Hold fast ___ to

kind - ness; your light shines _ for - ev - er and ev - er.

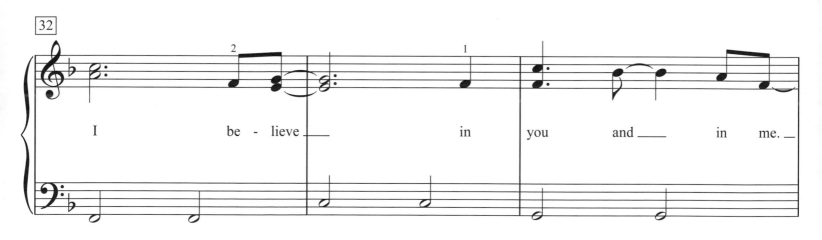

I be - lieve ___ in you and ___ in me. _

To Coda ⊕

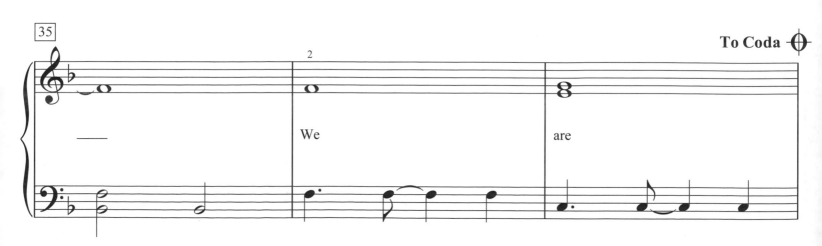

___ We are

D.S. al Coda

strong. _____ When ___ once up - on _____ a time, _____ in sto - ries and ___ in rhyme, _____ a mo - ment you ___ can shine ___ and wear your own ___ crown.

58

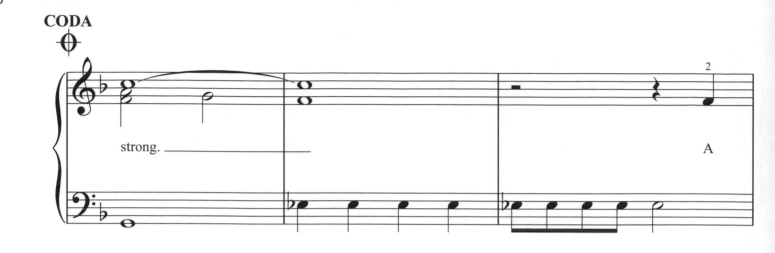

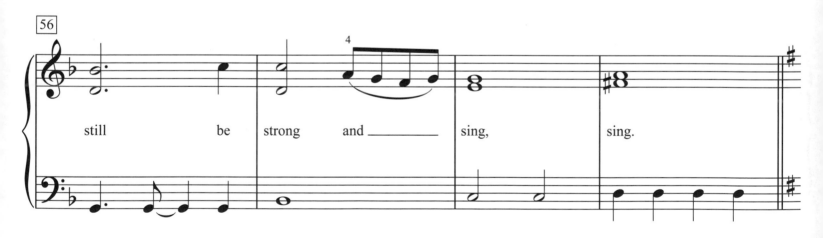

Hold fast ___ to kind - ness; your light shines ___ for-ev - er and ev - er.

I be - lieve ___ in you and ___ in me. ___

We are strong. ___

That's How You Know

from ENCHANTED

Music by ALAN MENKEN
Lyrics by STEPHEN SCHWARTZ

Freely

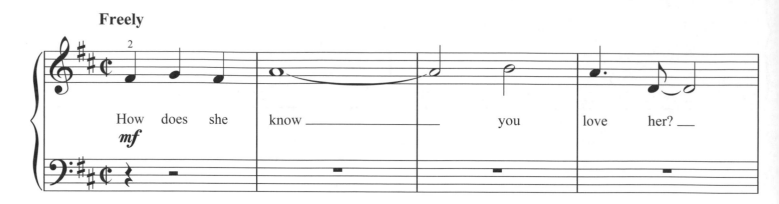

How does she know _____ you love her? ___

How does she know _____ she's yours?

Moderate Calypso

How does she know that you love her?

How do you show her you love her?

How does she know that you real - ly, real - ly, tru -

- ly love her? How does she know that you love her?

How do you show her you love her? How does she know

that you real - ly, real - ly, tru - ly love her?

It's not e-nough to take the one you love for grant-ed. _____

_____ You must re-mind her, or _____ she'll be in-clined to

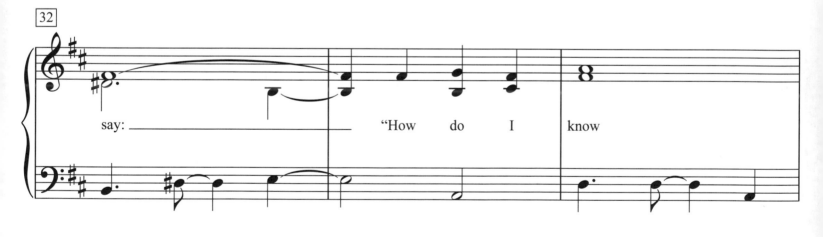

say: _____ "How do I know

he loves me? ___ How do I

know   he's   mine?"

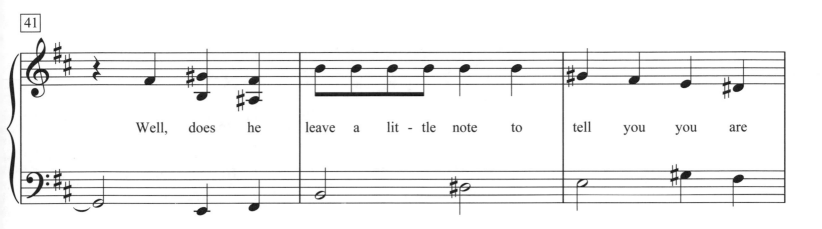

Well, does he   leave a lit - tle note to   tell   you   you   are

on   his   mind? ____   Send you yel - low flow - ers

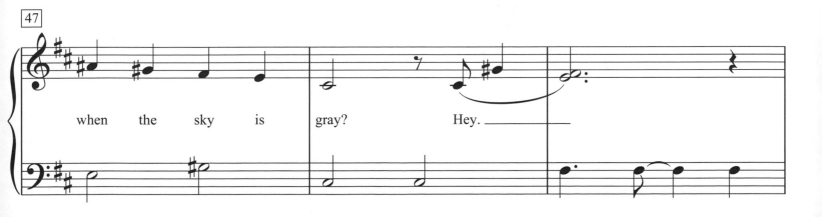

when   the   sky   is   gray?   Hey. ____

He'll find a new way to show you _____ a lit - tle bit ev - 'ry day. _____

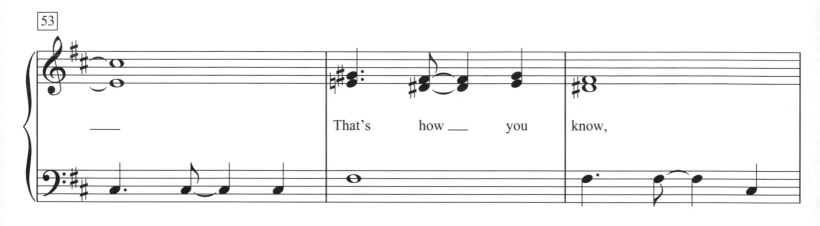

_____ That's how _____ you know,

that's how _____ you know he's _____ your love.

That's how you show her you love her.

You've got to show her you need her; don't treat her like

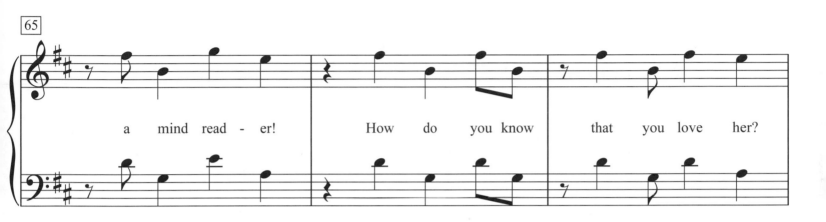

a mind read - er! How do you know that you love her?

That's how you know that you love her. It's not e - nough to take _

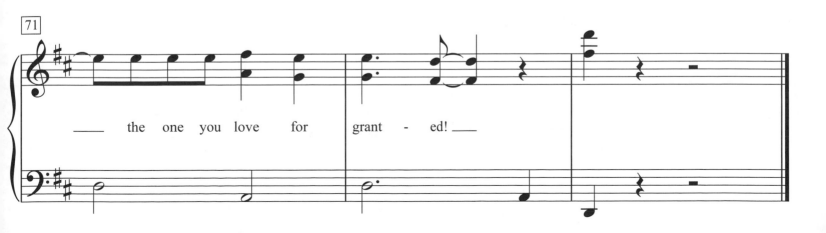

_ the one you love for grant - ed! _

Touch the Sky

from BRAVE

Music by ALEXANDER L. MANDEL
Lyrics by ALEXANDER L. MANDEL
and MARK ANDREWS

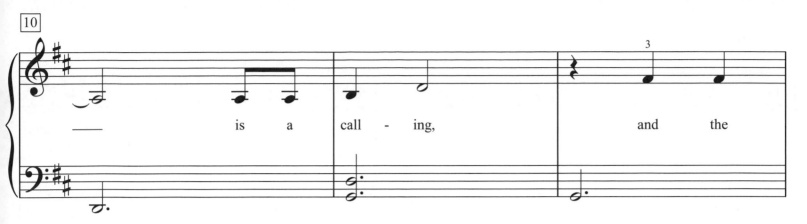

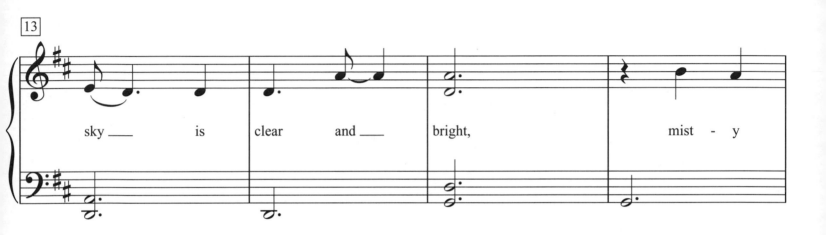

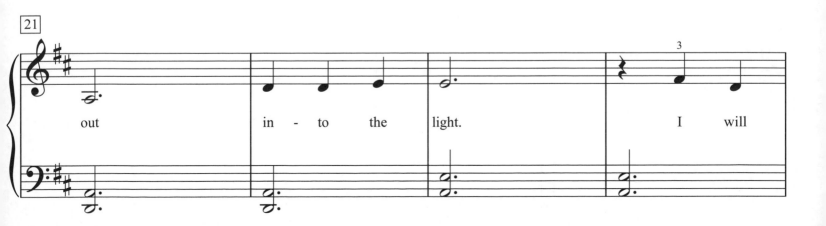

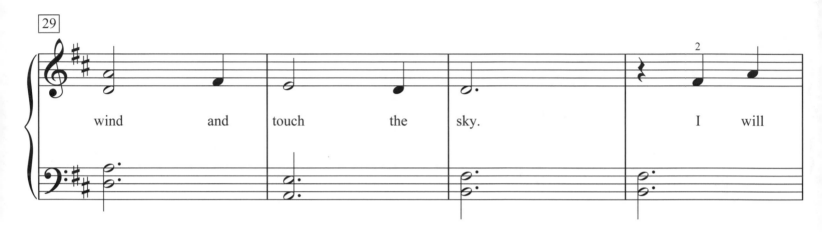

69

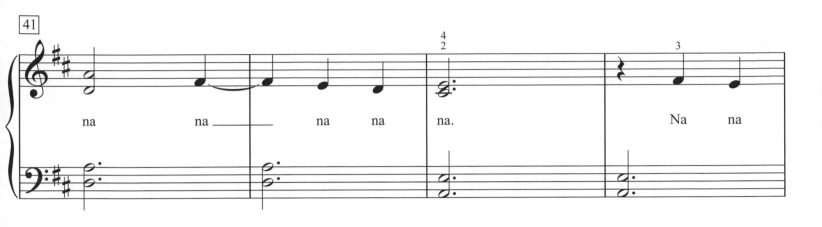

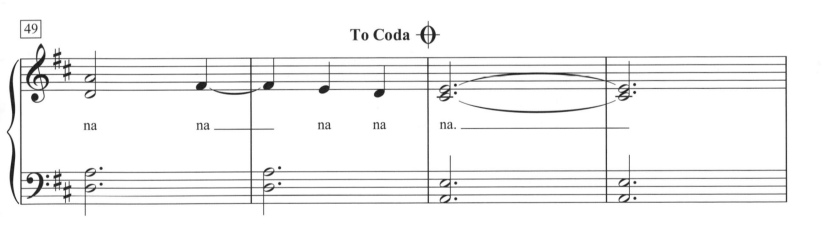

To Coda ⊕

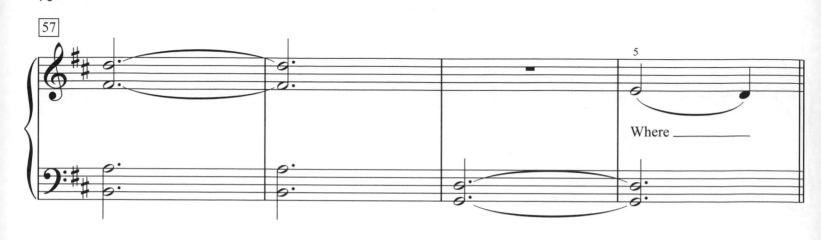

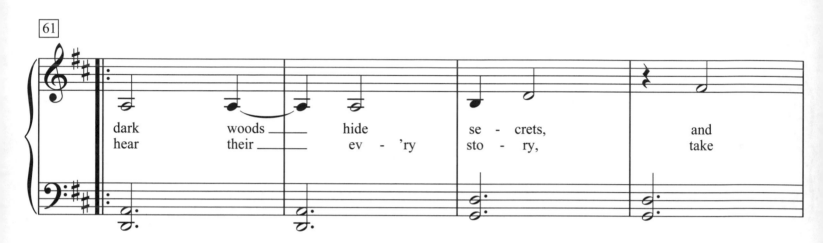

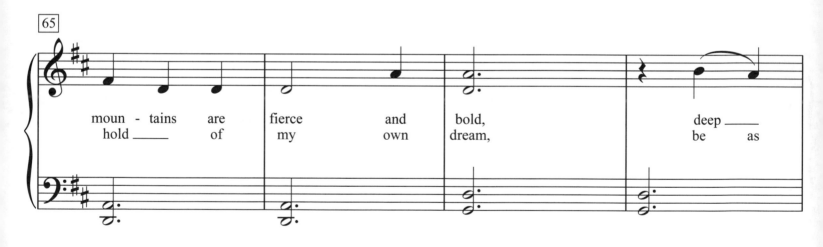

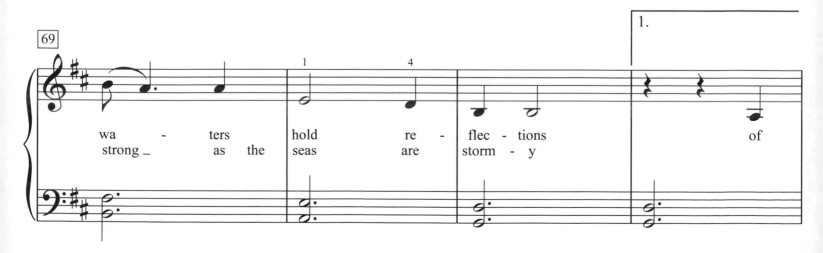

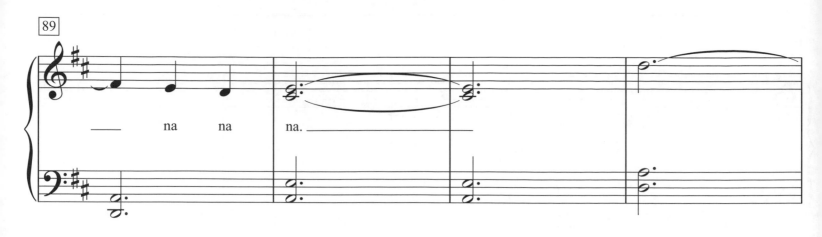

na na na.

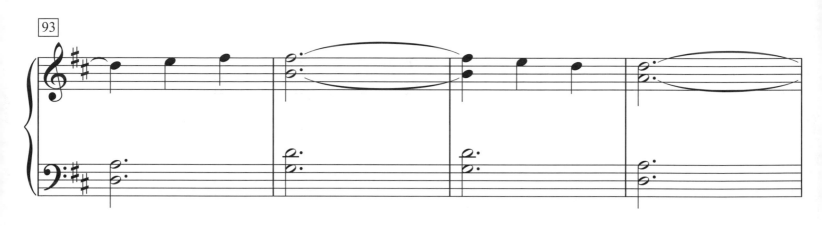

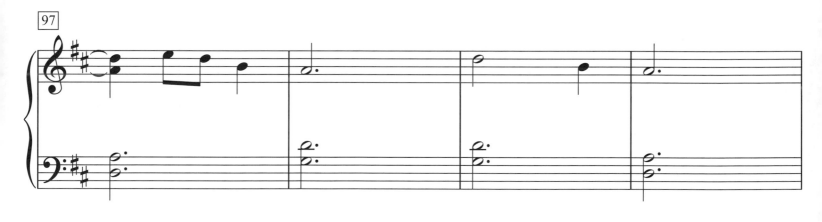

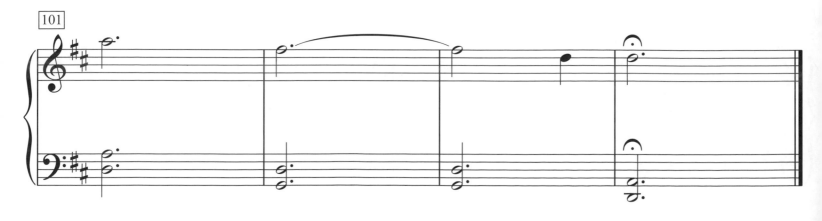

When Will My Life Begin?

from TANGLED

Music by ALAN MENKEN
Lyrics by GLENN SLATER

Moderately fast

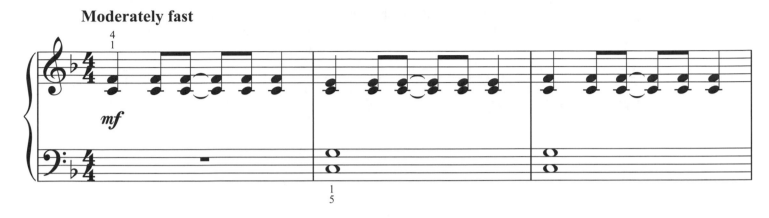

Rapunzel: Sev - en a. m., ___ the u - su - al morn - ing
Then af - ter lunch, it's puz - zles, and darts and

line - up. ___ Start on the chores, ___ and sweep ___ 'til the floor's all
bak - ing... ___ pa - per mâ - ché, ___ a bit ___ of bal - let and

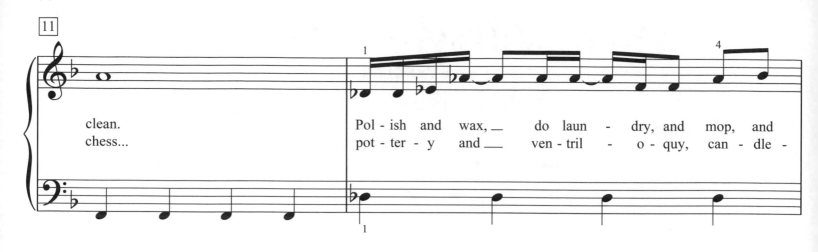

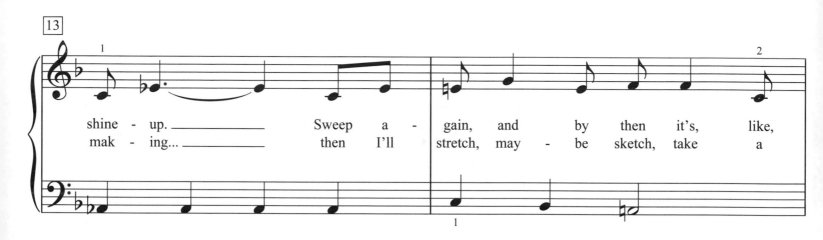

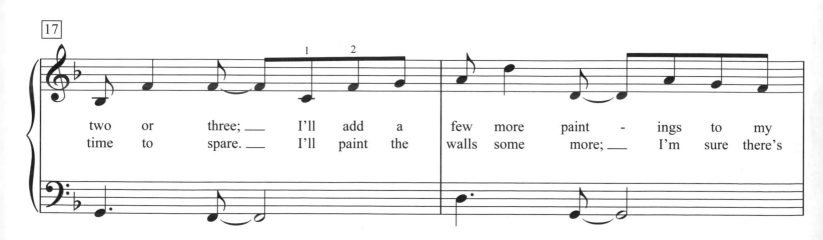

same place I've al - ways _____ been, _____ and I'll keep

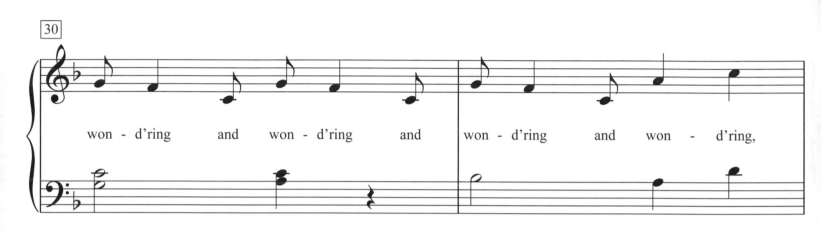

won - d'ring and won - d'ring and won - d'ring and won - d'ring,

Slowly, freely

"When will my life be - gin?" To - mor - row night... _

_____ the lights will ___ ap - pear,

just   like   they   do   on ____ my   birth - day ____ each

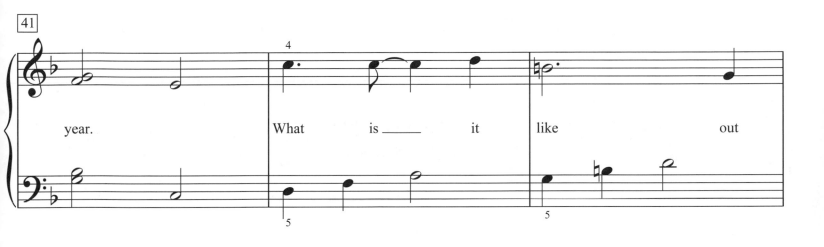

year.   What   is ____ it   like   out

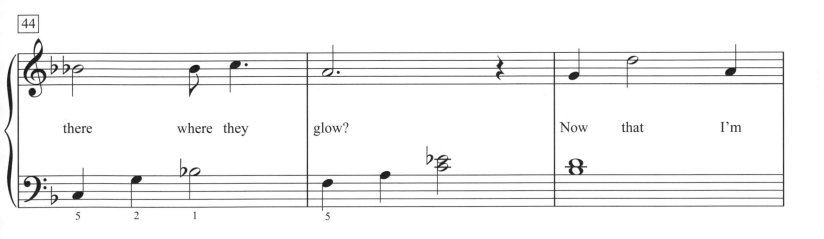

there   where they   glow?   Now   that   I'm

old - er, ____ Moth - er   might   just   let   me   go...

A Whole New World
from ALADDIN

Music by ALAN MENKEN
Lyrics by TIM RICE

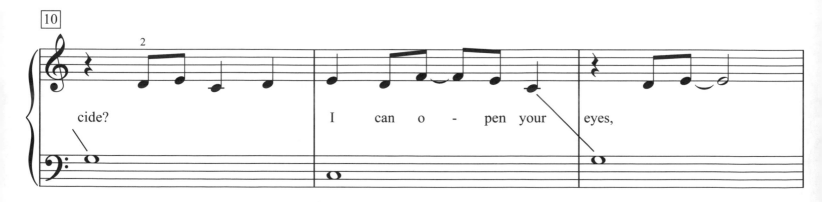

take you won - der by won - der, o - ver, side - ways and

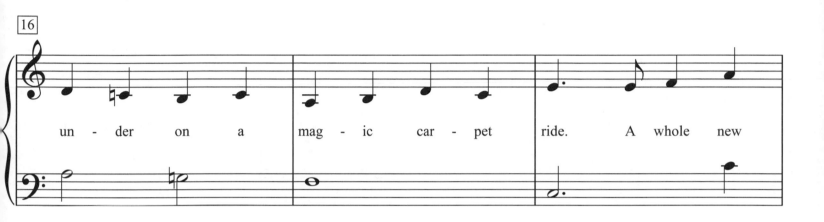

un - der on a mag - ic car - pet ride. A whole new

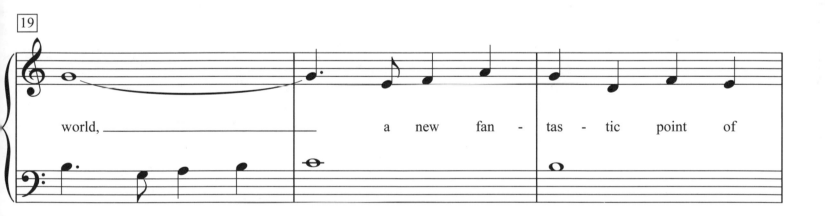

world, _____ a new fan - tas - tic point of

view. No one to tell us no, or where to go or

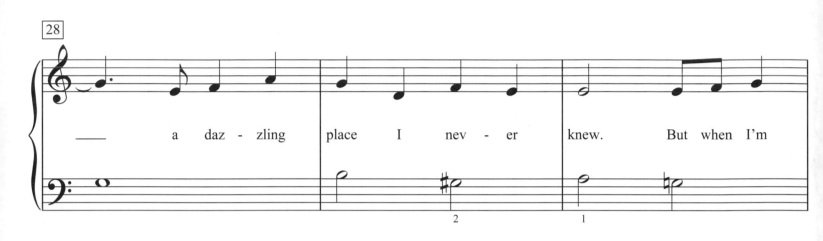

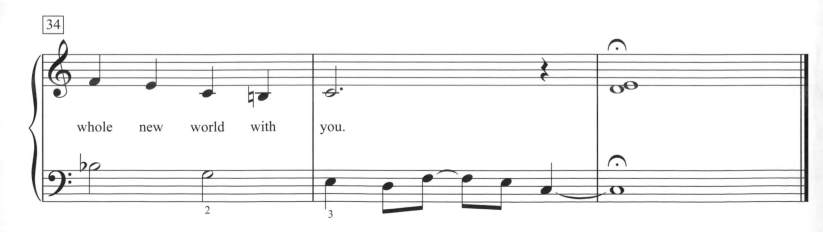

You're Welcome
from MOANA

Music and Lyrics by
LIN-MANUEL MIRANDA

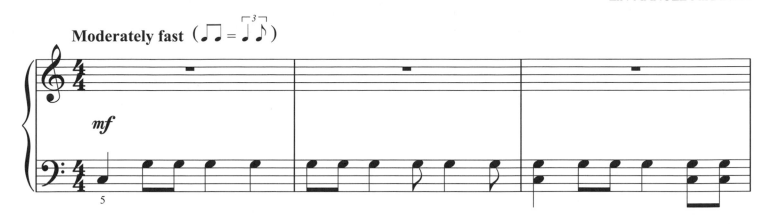

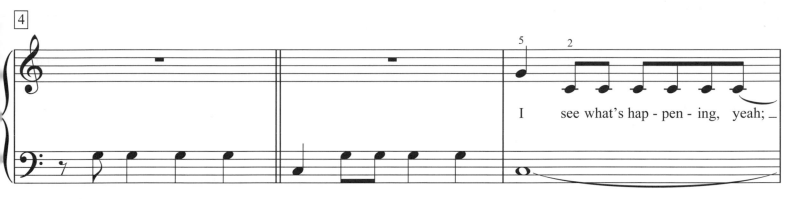

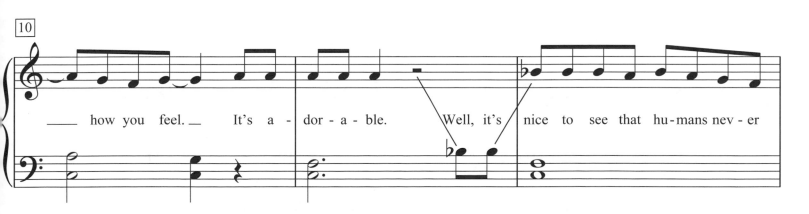

change.   O - pen your eyes. __   Let's __ be - gin. __   Yes, it's real - ly

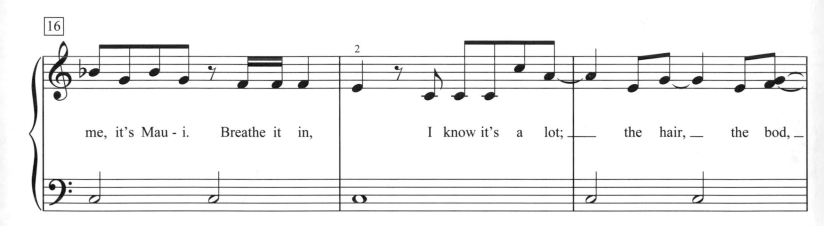

me, it's Mau - i.   Breathe it in,   I know it's a lot; __ the hair, __ the bod, __

__ when you're star - ing at a dem - i - god. __   What can I say __

__ ex - cept, "You're wel - come,   for the tides, __ the sun, __ the sky?" __

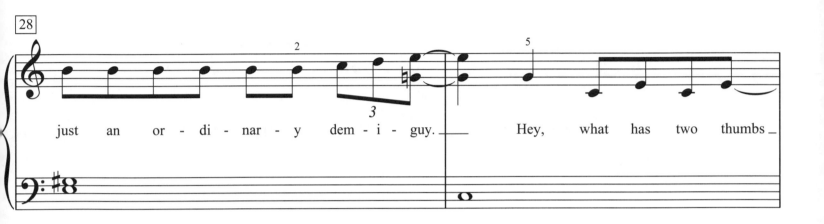

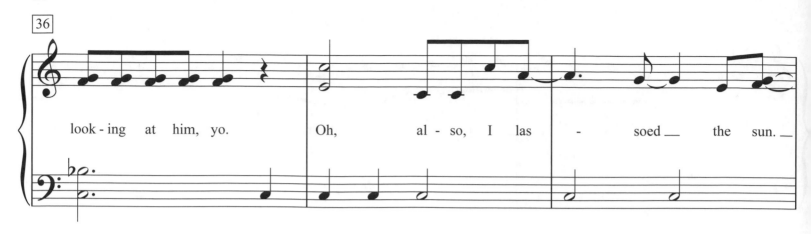

ex - cept, __ "You're wel - come, for the is - lands I pulled from the sea?" __

__ There's no need to pray, __ it's o - kay, __ you're wel - come. Huh! I

guess it's just my way of be - ing me! ____ You're wel - come! You're wel -

- come! And thank you.

8vb

You'll Be in My Heart*
(Pop Version)
from TARZAN®

Words and Music by
PHIL COLLINS

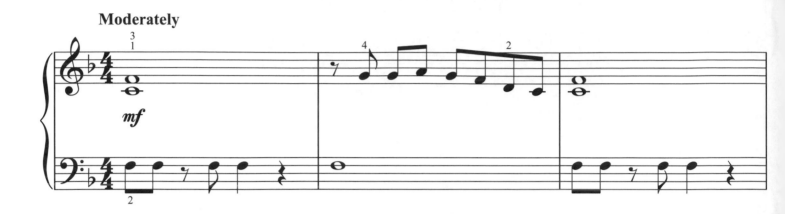

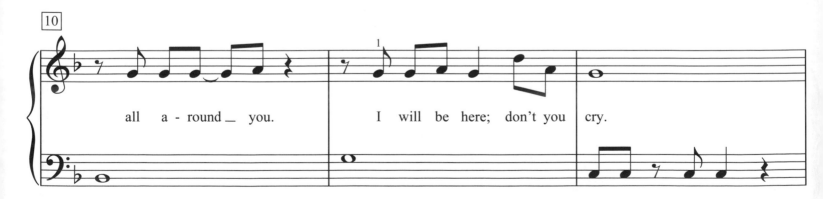

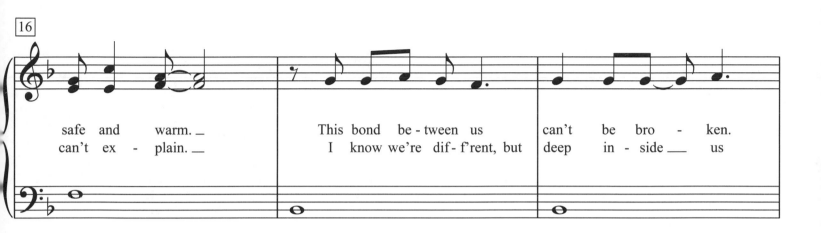

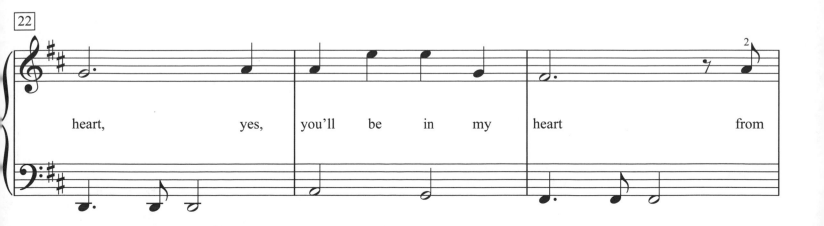

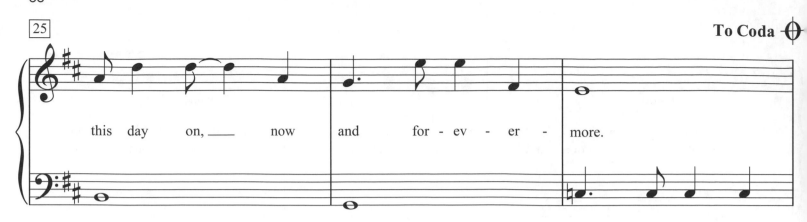

To Coda ⊕

this day on, ___ now and for - ev - er - more.

You'll be in my heart no

mat - ter what they say. You'll be here in ___ my

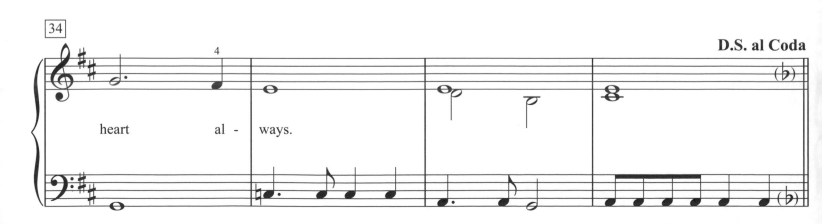

D.S. al Coda

heart al - ways.

CODA

Don't lis - ten to them, ___ 'cause
des - ti - ny calls you, you

what do they know? _ We
must _ be strong. _ It
need each oth - er to
may not be with you,
have, to hold. —
but you've got to hold on. —
They'll

1.

see in time, ___
I know. ___
When

2.

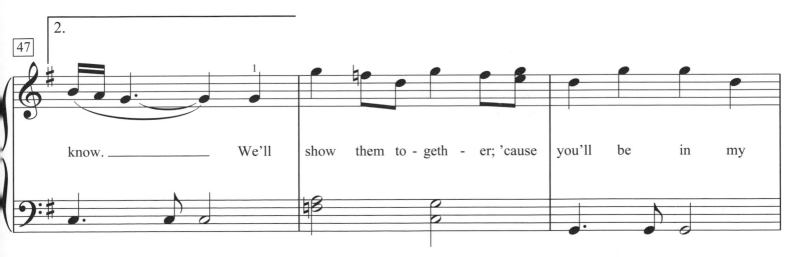

know. ___ We'll show them to - geth - er; 'cause you'll be in my

heart.   Be - lieve me,   you'll   be   in   my   heart.   I'll   be   there from

this day   on, ___   now _   and   for - ev - er - more.

You'll   be   in   my   heart   no   mat - ter   what   they   say.   You'll

be   here   in ___   my   heart   al -   ways.   Al - ways. _

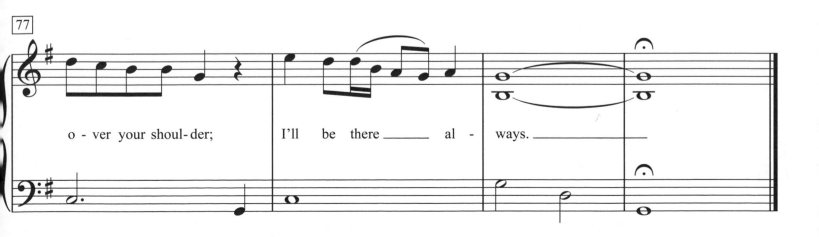

You've Got a Friend in Me

from TOY STORY

Music and Lyrics by
RANDY NEWMAN

You've got   a   friend   in   me.
You've got   a   friend   in   me.

You've got   a   friend   in   me.
You've got   a   friend   in   me.

When the   road   looks
You   got   trou - bles,   then

rough   a - head____   and   you're   miles____   and   miles____   from   your
I   got   'em   too.____   There   is - n't   an - y - thing

94

Now some oth - er folks might be a lit - tle bit smart - er than I am,

big - ger and strong - er too. May - be. But none of them will

ev - er love you the way I do, just me and you, ___ boy.

And as the years go by, our friend - ship will nev - er

die.

You're gon - na see it's our des - ti - ny.

You've got a friend in me.

You've got a friend in me.

You've got a friend in me.

rit.